Standard Vocal Literature

Soprano

Edited by Richard Walters

Editions of some of the songs and arias in this collection, including historical notes and translations, were previously published in the following Hal Leonard Vocal Library titles:

English Songs: Renaissance to Baroque
Edited by Steven Stolen and Richard Walters

Roger Quilter: 55 Songs
Edited by Richard Walters

The French Song Anthology
Edited by Carol Kimball and Richard Walters

The Lieder Anthology
Edited by Virginia Saya and Richard Walters

Anthology of Spanish Song
Edited by Maria DiPalma and Richard Walters

Gilbert & Sullivan for Singers
Edited by Richard Walters

The Oratorio Anthology
Edited by Richard Walters

The realizations are by the editor unless noted.

Cover painting: Vincent van Gogh, *The Starry Night*, Oil on canvas, 29 x 36¼", 1889

ISBN 0-634-07873-9

HAL•LEONARD®
CORPORATION
7777 W. BLUEMOUND RD. P.O. BOX 13819 MILWAUKEE, WI 53213

Visit Hal Leonard Online at
www.halleonard.com

Preface

In a constant study of collections available for voice I noticed few which attempt a comprehensive sweep of repertoire in different languages. There are admittedly some cornerstone publications addressing diverse pre-standard or teaching literature, incidentally touching on music by major vocal composers, but these are for student singers at a remedial level. *Standard Vocal Literature* addresses the needs of a typical college singer who has moved beyond teaching literature, but is perhaps not yet ready for a deeper look into a particular genre of song or the work of a single composer. Of course, the singer for whom this collection is a perfect fit need not be a college student. He or she also might be an advanced high school student, or an adult studying classical voice.

The principal aim of the collection is to introduce art song in five languages. The compilation plan is as follows:

- ten songs in English, representing Renaissance and Baroque music by Dowland, Purcell and others, as well as romantic song of the late 19th and early 20th centuries by Quilter, Vaughan Williams and others

- four songs in French, with special emphasis on the songs of Fauré

- six songs in German, with a sampling of music by the greatest lieder composers: Schubert, Schumann, Brahms, Strauss

- four songs in Italian that branch out beyond the standard early Italian songs students are likely to already be studying, with the deliberate inclusion of music by Bellini to get a taste of bel canto, and Stephano Donaudy, for a broader Italian romanticism

- two songs in Spanish by principal composers

Songs have been chosen with particular voice types in mind, presented in appropriate keys. Beyond art song, the collection includes:

- two opera arias, chosen from the first pieces that most singers study

- one operetta aria by Gilbert & Sullivan

- one oratorio aria as an introduction to the field

In addition to those specific parameters, we made certain that music by Mozart appears in each volume, which many would agree is the very best instruction in beautiful singing.

Because it is so important for students to learn an artistic context for music and poetry, we have provided introductory articles for all songs, including biographical and historical information that could be a springboard for more detailed research. To complete the package, we have recorded carefully prepared piano accompaniments to aid practice, and pronunciation lessons to assist in learning songs.

Each of the 30 selections in this volume is a gem in its own right. May they be the beginning of a lifelong discovery of our great heritage of vocal art music.

Richard Walters
Editor
October, 2004

Contents

Composer Index

About the Accompaniment Recordings...

Our accompaniment recordings are intended as an educational tool in learning a song. We take great care to produce excellent recordings with a pianist very experienced in accompanying singers in song literature. However, it is important that teachers and singers apply insight in the use of these recordings. There is no one ideal tempo for any song. By necessity we have chosen a tempo for recording which we believe reasonably represents each song. Each singer, working with a pianist, will find his or her own best tempo to bring a song to life in rehearsals and live performance. You may find that you need a slightly slower or faster tempo. You also may find your own ideas of rubato and other slight breaks in the tempo as you create your own interpretation. Above all, do not allow yourself or your students to build a rather robotic rendition of a song as a slave to the recorded accompaniment. Remember that the purpose of art song is a personal expression reflecting something real about humanity.

About the Pronunciation Recordings...

In our recordings of French and German we have used a native speaker, which we think will be most instructive. However, it is crucial to note that the guttural pronunciation of "R" in French and German on the recordings, accurate for spoken diction, needs to be modified in classical singing to a rolled or flipped "R" in German, depending on context, and generally to a flipped "R" in French. We encourage you to listen to the many available recordings of famous singers of French and German song as models in this regard.

CD Contents

Laura Ward, pianist

CD 1

Songs in English
1 Blow, blow thou winter wind
2 Where the bee sucks
3 Come again, sweet love
4 Flow my tears
5 The Silver Swan
6 I attempt from love's sickness
7 If music be the food of love
8 It was a lover and his lass
9 Love's Philosophy
10 Weep you no more

Songs in French
Après un rêve[1]
11 Recitation
12 Pronunciation Lesson
13 Accompaniment
Chanson d'amour[2]
14 Recitation
15 Pronunciation Lesson
16 Accompaniment
Si mes vers avaient des ailes[2]
17 Recitation
18 Pronunciation Lesson
19 Accompaniment
Plaisir d'amour[2]
20 Recitation
21 Pronunciation Lesson
22 Accompaniment

Songs in German
Vergebliches Ständchen[4]
23 Recitation
24 Pronunciation Lesson
25 Accompaniment
Wie Melodien zieht es mir[3]
26 Recitation
27 Pronunciation Lesson
28 Accompaniment
Das Veilchen[4]
29 Recitation
30 Pronunciation Lesson
31 Accompaniment
Du bist die Ruh[4]
32 Recitation
33 Pronunciation Lesson
34 Accompaniment
Gretchen am Spinnrade[4]
35 Recitation
36 Pronunciation Lesson
37 Accompaniment

CD 2

Songs in German continued from CD 1
Breit' über mein Haupt[4]
1 Recitation
2 Pronunciation Lesson
3 Accompaniment

Songs in Italian
L'abbandono
4 Recitation
5 Pronunciation Lesson
6 Accompaniment
Intorno all'idol mio
7 Recitation
8 Pronunciation Lesson
9 Accompaniment
Come l'allodoletta
10 Recitation
11 Pronunciation Lesson
12 Accompaniment
Ridente la calma
13 Recitation
14 Pronunciation Lesson
15 Accompaniment

Songs in Spanish
El majo discreto[5]
16 Recitation
17 Pronunciation Lesson
18 Accompaniment
Del cabello más sutil[6]
19 Recitation
20 Pronunciation Lesson
21 Accompaniment

Opera arias
Deh vieni, non tardar
22 Recitation
23 Pronunciation Lesson
24 Accompaniment
O mio babbino caro
25 Recitation
26 Pronunciation Lesson
27 Accompaniment

Operetta aria
28 The Sun, Whose Rays Are All Ablaze

Oratorio aria
Pie Jesu
29 Recitation
30 Pronunciation Lesson
31 Accompaniment

Language Coaches:

French [1] Nicole Chandler [2] Bernard Zinck   **German** [3] Johanna Moore [4] Elisabeth Witte
Italian and Latin Martha Gerhart   **Spanish** [5] Emma Acevedo [6] Rose Rodriguez

Thomas Arne

Thomas Arne was the son of an upholsterer, coffin maker, and erstwhile Handel opera producer. He was part of a colorful and musical family. Arne was born in London on or around March 12, 1710, and baptized on May 28, 1710. As a youth, Thomas smuggled a spinet into his room and muffled the strings with a handkerchief to avoid waking the rest of the family with his secret practicing. He disguised himself as a liveryman to gain access to the gallery at the Italian Opera. Following his schooling, Arne pursued a legal career for a short time until his father discovered his musical aspirations. He was ultimately allowed to abandon law to pursue a life in music. Arne gave his sister and younger brother voice lessons, and together with his siblings presented a performance of Handel's *Acis and Galatea* at London's Haymarket Theatre in 1732. Arne played the lute and violin and was a self-taught composer. He had strong interest in the stage and had tremendous success as a composer of operas and masques. The song "Rule, Britannia" is from his masque *Alfred*, written in 1740. Other notable compositions include *Rosamond* (1733), *Dido and Aeneas* (1733), *Comus* (1738), some 25 books of songs, and numerous instrumental works, often featuring organ or harpsichord. In 1744 he was appointed resident composer at the Drury Lane Theatre in London and held that post until a disagreement with a performer prompted him to leave for Covent Garden in 1760. Arne received particular attention and acclaim at Drury Lane for his settings of Shakespearean texts, two of which are included in this collection. He received an honorary doctorate from Oxford in 1759, hence the often-used title of Doctor Arne. Arne also composed oratorios, though was never as successful as his contemporary, George Frideric Handel. Arne's principal gift as a composer was a sure sense of melody. He died on March 5, 1778.

Blow, blow thou winter wind

During Arne's tenure at the Drury Lane Theatre, he composed incidental music and songs for Shakespeare plays, including *As You Like It*, *The Merchant of Venice*, *Much Ado about Nothing*, *The Tempest* and *Twelfth Night*. "Blow, blow thou winter wind" was written for a production of *As You Like It*, premiered at Drury Lane on December 20, 1740. It occurs in the play during Act II, scene 7. Other notable English composers have set this text, including Frank Bridge (in 1903), Sir Hubert Parry (in 1885) and Roger Quilter (in 1905).

Where the bee sucks

In 1740 Arne composed incidental music and songs for Shakespeare's *The Tempest*. This production premiered at Drury Lane on November 28, 1740, and was later revived in 1746. It is possible that "Where the bee sucks" was composed for these performances. In the play this text appears in Act V, scene 1. Other composers to set this text include Frederic Ayres, John Banister, Lukas Foss, Arthur Honegger (in French), Robert Johnson, and Michael Tippett.

2. Where the bee sucks 2:20

William Shakespeare
(1564-1616)
from *The Tempest*

Thomas Arne
(1710-1778)

1. Blow, blow thou winter wind

William Shakespeare
(1564-1616)
from *As You Like It*

Thomas Arne
(1710-1778)

* In each of the verses, the two large sections
(measures 9-16, measures 17-32) may each be repeated.

Come again, sweet love

Anonymous

John Dowland
(1563-1626)

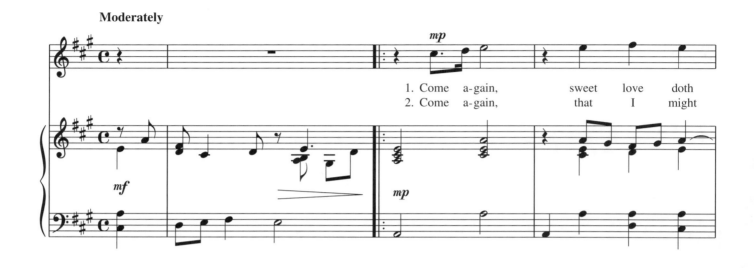

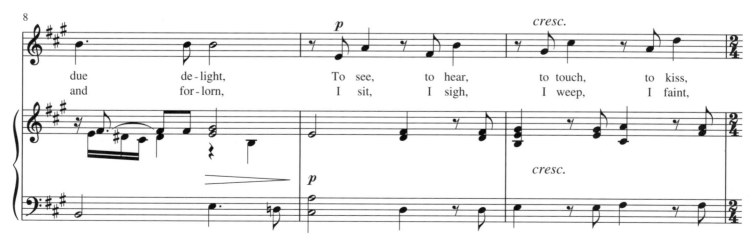

* Small size notes are optional for verse two.
The commentary for this song appears on page 16.

Flow my tears

Anonymous

John Dowland
(1563-1626)

[Slow]

[mp]

Flow my _ tears fall _____ from your springs, Ex - il'd _____
Down vain _ lights shine _____ you no more, No nights ___

___ for - ev - er let me mourn: Where night's black bird her
___ are dark e - nough for those That in de - spair their

sad in - fa - my sings, There let me live _____ for - lorn.
last for - tunes de - plore, Light doth but shame _____ dis - close.

Nev - er may my woes_____ be re - liev - ed, Since pit - y is fled,
From the high - est spire_____ of _ con - tent - ment, My for - tune is thrown,

The commentary for this song appears on page 16.

John Dowland

Englishman John Dowland stands at the forefront of early composers of what could be loosely defined as art song with the creation or invention of the "ayre." The ayre is a simple form where the primary interest is in the top voice. The other voices are usually written in harmonizing choral style and could have been sung in that fashion, but were preferably performed by solo voice and lute. Dowland was both a singer and lutenist and traveled widely, performing his music and learning about art and style throughout Europe. His early years were marked by a period of service in Paris, working for the English ambassador, Henry Dobham. In 1580, while in Dobham's service, Dowland converted to Roman Catholicism. He returned to England in 1584, married, and tried to gain a position in Elizabeth's court. Unsuccessful, he began a period of travel that lasted until 1609, including time in Germany and Italy. Near the end of the century, Dowland returned both to Protestantism and to England, but again was unsuccessful professionally, so he went to Denmark as court musician to Christian IV in 1598. Dowland often complained that his lack of success in England was because of his acceptance abroad. It was, however, his cosmopolitan background that made his music widely known and gave it such lasting impact. His works include three volumes of lute songs (1597-1603), a set of instrumental pavans entitled *Lachrymae*, and a collection of songs with viol and lute accompaniment, *A Pilgrim's Solace*.

The songs of Dowland demonstrate his musical prowess. Early songs were generally strophic in form, with very memorable melodies, but restrained harmony. In later songs, Dowland ventured away from strophic form, choosing to through-compose to better illustrate the emotional content of the lyrics. His melodies echo the rhythm and meaning of speech. A higher degree of chromaticism and discord between the lute and the voice also serve to heighten the most dramatic and tragic parts of his songs. Dowland showed a true sense of poetry in his choice of texts, the authors of which are primarily unknown. It is possible that Dowland wrote some of the song texts himself. His songs certainly reflect the Shakespearian spirit of the era. "Come again, sweet love" dates from 1597. "Flow my tears" was written in 1600.

Orlando Gibbons

Englishman Orlando Gibbons came from a musical family in Oxford. His grandfather, Richard, was a chamberlain of the city, and his father, William, was well known as a musician. At the age of 12, Orlando joined the choir at King's College, Cambridge, where his brother Edward was master of the choristers. In 1605 he was appointed organist at the Chapel Royal and held this position until his death. Oxford awarded him a doctorate in 1622, and he was appointed organist at Westminster Abbey the following year. Most notable as a keyboard player and composer for harpsichord and organ, and for his service music and anthems, Gibbons was also a fine writer of madrigals in the traditional style. He died suddenly at Canterbury on June 5, 1625 while waiting to render his services at the marriage of Charles I.

The Silver Swan

Gibbons left only 13 madrigals in a published collection (1612). Although originally written in five-part choral form, "The Silver Swan" is also performed as a solo song in the tradition of the lute ayre. The philosophic poetry of the text and its noble melody easily make "The Silver Swan" Gibbons' most famous composition.

The Silver Swan

Anonymous

Orlando Gibbons
(1583-1625)

I attempt from love's sickness

from
THE INDIAN QUEEN

Henry Purcell
(1659-1695)

The commentary on this song appears on page 26.

* optional melodic ornamentation by the editors
** appoggiatura possible

22

If music be the food of love
(First Version)

Colonel Henry Heveningham

Henry Purcell
(1659-1695)

The commentary for this song appears on page 26.

* appoggiatura possible
** optional melodic ornamentation by the editors

Henry Purcell

From the time of John Dowland to the notable figures of the 20th century, Henry Purcell stands alone as the greatest British composer, and his death in 1695 marked the end of any important musical contribution from an English-born composer for nearly 200 years. Like many of his contemporaries, he came from a musical family, which included his brother Daniel, an important composer of the period as well. Henry was a chorister at the Chapel Royal at the age of 10. In 1673 he left this position and began his study with John Blow, succeeding him in 1679 as organist at Westminster Abbey. In these first years at the Abbey, Purcell began composing in earnest and wrote his first music for a play, Nathanial Lee's *Theodosius*. He went on to write music and songs for over 50 dramatic works. *Dido and Aeneas* (1689) was written for a production at a girl's school and was his only through-composed opera. Despite its humble origins, this is the first great opera in the English language. In it Purcell invented an original style of accompanied recitative, something never before composed in English. The opera remains the only representative of the period still being performed as a regular part of the repertory today. Other operatic and semi-operatic works include *King Arthur* (1691), *The Fairy Queen* (1692), and *The Indian Queen* (1695).

Purcell's other notable appointments during his brief life include service in 1682 as a Gentleman of the Chapel Royal, where he sang bass and served as one of three organists. He also became the Royal Repairman in 1683, to oversee the new organ at Temple Church. In 1685 James II named him Royal Harpsichordist. Despite these court appointments, Purcell depended greatly on the theater for income. He also composed a large amount of church and service music, including the music for the funeral of Queen Mary in 1694. This music was performed at his own funeral just one year later. His vocal music includes the ode for St. Cecilia's Day *Hail, Bright Cecilia* (1692) and the songs in *Orpheus Britannicus*, a two-volume collection published after his death. He also wrote *Nine Fantasias* (1680), *Twelve Sonatas of Three Parts* (1683), *Musick's Handmaid* (1689) for harpsichord, and another collection published posthumously, *Lessons for the Harpsichord or Spinet, Suites No. 1-8*. Little is known about Purcell's life in the 1690s. He suffered death from illness, but the nature is not known. Purcell was buried in Westminster Abbey as an honored British citizen. Of his seven children, only two were known to survive into adulthood.

I attempt from love's sickness

The Indian Queen, a "semi-opera" with a libretto by John Dryden and R. Howard, was produced at the Drury Lane Theatre in London in 1695. Theatre in England during the Restoration period valued a love of the spoken word. An operatic theatrical style, as in France and Italy, was not yet welcome in London. However in five "semi-operas" Purcell was able to write fairly substantial scores. Had he lived longer, he might have been given the opportunity to develop opera on the professional London stage.

If music be the food of love (First version)

"If music be the food of love" was first published in 1692 in *The Gentleman's Journal: or The Monthly Miscellany*, a magazine started by a young Huguenot refugee, Pierre Antoine Motteux. This is the first of three versions Purcell wrote between 1692 and 1695. The opening line is Shakespeare; the remainder of the text is the work of a Suffolk gentleman, Colonel Henry Heveningham. While Purcell was writing vocal music in a primarily Italianate style during the 1690s, the first version of "If music be the food of love" is an air in traditional English style. In contrast, Purcell shows a pronounced Italian influence in his third setting of this text, written in 1695.

Roger Quilter

Roger Quilter was a breed of composer that has rarely existed after the first decades of the 20th century: he was overwhelmingly concerned with the art song. His preoccupation with the genre spanned from his youth until near his death, more than 50 years later, resulting in roughly 140 songs in total.

Quilter was born into a wealthy family in Sussex, England. He went abroad to study composition with Ivann Knorr in Frankfurt at the Hoch Conservatory. It was here that he met lifelong close friend Percy Grainger. A public career began for Quilter with the 1901 London premiere of *Songs of the Sea*, not surprisingly the composer's choice for the designation of Opus 1. Gervase Elwes, a celebrated tenor, became interested in Quilter's songs. For him the composer wrote the song cycle *To Julia*, which Elwes premiered in 1905. The same singer gave the first performance of the *Seven Elizabethan Lyrics* in 1908. Quilter's music soon gained favor, and his songs were regularly performed, particularly in London. A good pianist, the composer often served as an accompanist in London during the first decades of the 20th century.

Due to inheritance, Quilter never had to work, leaving his time and mind free for composing, though his life was not always a happy one. His wealth was limited, and in later years he was often in debt. He was plagued by chronic poor health, which prevented military service during World War I. Quilter was a well-mannered, sophisticated gentleman, with the polish of his well-to-do social class. He suffered unstable periods, with pronounced mental illness in the years leading to his death. He never married, though he formed a few close attachments and had devoted friends and supporters.

Quilter valued graceful elegance and a love of words, both qualities that are evident in his songs and his idiomatic phrasing for the voice. The imagery in his songs reflects his boyhood countryside of southern England. He was uninterested in the more extreme and progressive artistic trends of the 20th century. In general, though there are exceptions, he showed a rather refined literary taste in poetry chosen for his songs, with an inherent nationalistic British identification. Quilter's fluid and distinctive musical style, though occasionally dramatic, is most often infused with a natural, creamy English charm, though he did not compose quickly, and labored over every detail. Most agree that his best work was created rather young in his life, before his mid-40s.

Today Quilter would be considered a minor historical figure in British music overall. Regarding art song, however, very few composers working in English have matched his achievement of a living body of beloved, relevant, literate repertoire.

It was a lover and his lass
from *Five Shakespeare Songs*, Op. 23 (Second Set)

Original key: E major. Three of the songs in this set were composed in 1919. "Fear no more" was composed in 1921. "It was a lover and his lass" was originally composed as a duet in 1919; the solo version was composed in 1921. Unlike the Shakespeare songs of Op. 6, which are conceptually linked, this opus is simply a collection of songs. Three of the songs were dedicated to Quilter's close friend Walter Creighton, a singer in his youth and the artist who premiered Ralph Vaughan Williams' *Songs of Travel*. The songs have been often recorded.

Love's Philosophy
from *Three Songs*, Op. 3

Original key. Composed c.1905. Probably first performed by tenor Gervase Elwes, to whom the song is dedicated, with Quilter as pianist. Published by Boosey and Co., 1905. Published by Schott in German translation, 1924. Elwes (1866-1921) was a celebrated concert singer, and Quilter's favorite. Elwes' voice was not especially large, but was well suited to recital. He sang with clarity, finesse and sensitivity. This is one of the most recorded of Quilter's songs.

Weep you no more
from *Seven Elizabethan Lyrics*, Op. 12

Original key. Composed 1907. First performance most likely by tenor Gervase Elwes and Roger Quilter, November 17, 1908, Bechstein Hall, London. Published as a set by Boosey and Co., 1908. Quilter rejected two songs originally composed for the set and wrote two new songs before the premiere. The texts for these songs had been variously published in collections. The set was dedicated to the memory of Gervase Elwes' mother, Alice Cary-Elwes, who died in 1907. The set and its individual songs have been recorded by several artists; "Weep you no more" is one of the most recorded. Quilter made various arrangements of the song.

To Walter Creighton

It was a lover and his lass

from *Five Shakespeare Songs*, Op. 23 (Second Set)

William Shakespeare
(1564-1616)
from *As You Like It*

Roger Quilter
(1877-1953)

lov - ers love _ the spring. _____ And

there - fore take the pre - sent time, With a hey, and a ho, and a

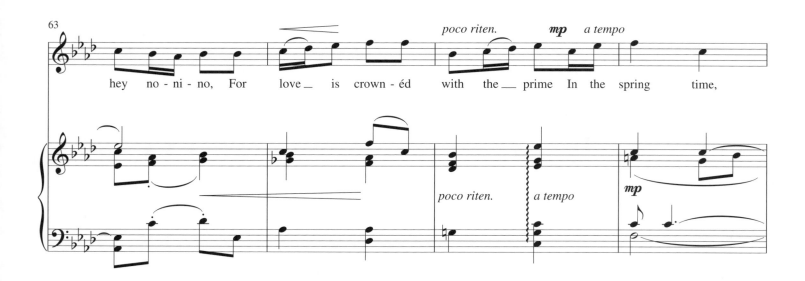

hey no - ni - no, For love _ is crown - éd with the _ prime In the spring time,

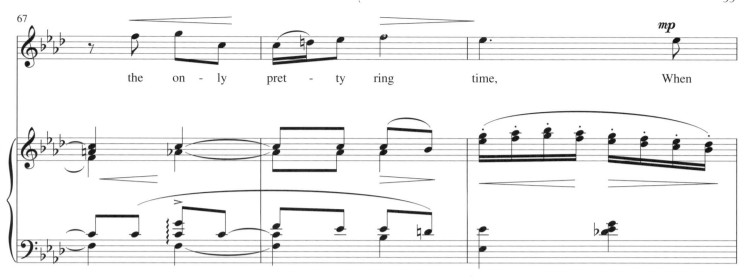

the on - ly pret - ty ring time, When

birds do sing, hey ding a ding, ding, ding a ding, ding,

ding a ding, ding; Sweet lov - ers love ___ the spring.

To the memory of my friend, Mrs. Cary-Elwes

Weep you no more

from *Seven Elizabethan Songs*, Op. 12

Anonymous

Roger Quilter
(1877-1953)

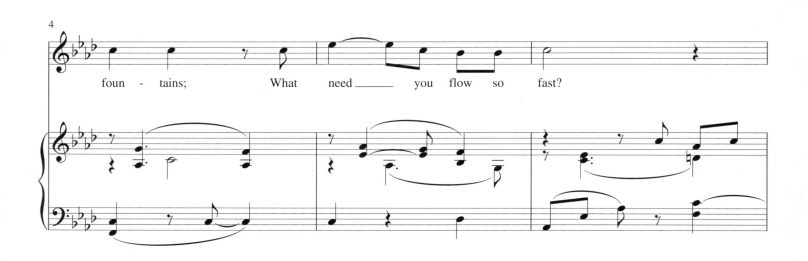

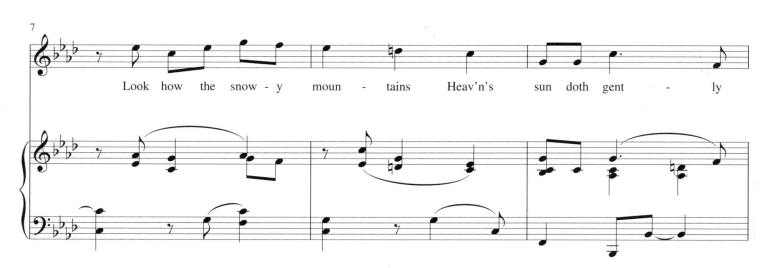

waste! But my Sun's heav'n-ly eyes _____ View not your

weep - ing, That now lies sleep - ing,

Soft - ly now soft - ly lies Sleep - ing,

sleep - ing.

Ped. *

To Gervase Elwes

Love's Philosophy
from *Three Songs*, Op. 3

Percy B. Shelley
(1792-1822)

Roger Quilter
(1877-1953)

Molto allegro con moto (♩ = 112)

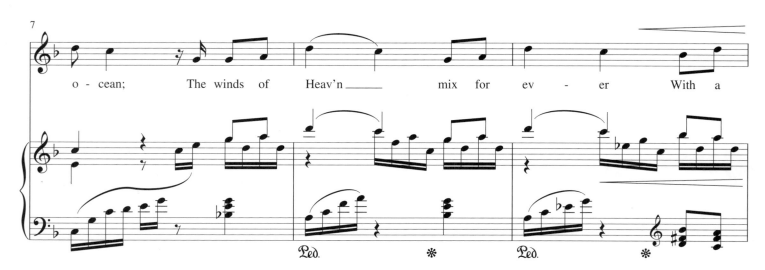

Gabriel Fauré

Frenchman Gabriel Fauré composed approximately 100 songs throughout his life. His first works for voice and piano date from his student days at the École Niedemeyer. At this point he was most attracted to the romantic poets, such as Victor Hugo. These early songs can be termed *romances*, and are generally strophic in form. Fauré's most important advance as a song composer with a more mature, personal style came with "Lydia," composed c.1870. In the 1880s he was drawn to the symbolists, the Parnassian poets and, most profoundly, to Paul Verlaine. The composer's song composition became bolder in the 1890s, evidenced by his cycle *La bonne chanson*. The music for voice composed in his later years, after the turn of the century (when Fauré began to suffer from deafness, probably due to arteriosclerosis), became more sparse and economical. He continued in his own highly personal compositional style, not following the dramatic changes in music brought on by Schoenberg, Stravinsky, and others, though he was well aware of their music (he was music critic for *Le Figaro* from 1903-1921), and most often admired it.

Fauré's songs were originally published in three collections of 20 songs each. (The second collection originally contained 25 songs, but upon the appearance of the third collection, recompilation occurred, putting the second collection back to 20 songs.) These collections were published by Hamelle, the first in 1879, the second in 1897, and the third in 1908. Prior to the publication of the first collection, some of Fauré's songs had been published individually, but Hamelle bought all previous rights. Fauré made very little money from his song compositions, and sold them outright for about 50 francs each for all publishing rights. The composition dates of the early songs are only approximate. His publisher asked him to retroactively assign opus numbers to the earlier songs upon their publication in the first collection of 1879. Fauré's memory was unclear about dates on many such songs. After publication he destroyed many manuscripts, so there are few clues for researchers. The tempo markings were Fauré's own, which he added at the point of publication.

Fauré worked slowly as a composer and was self-critical. He relied on the reactions of his colleagues and friends, mainly fellow composers with whom he was friendly. He admitted that at times he felt that his slow, painstaking approach to composition may have stifled spontaneity. In setting a poem, he didn't hesitate to omit verses or change words to suit his concept. Some of the small changes of words are undoubtedly oversight, but the majority were deliberate. He chose poems primarily for their pliability. Fauré said of his song composition, "seek above all to extricate the general feeling of a poem, rather than to concentrate on its details."

Harmony was Fauré's natural priority. His style was a fresh approach to tonal harmony, often freely using modes to achieve flow, fluency and ambiguity. Fauré was certainly a great melodist, but his melodies grow from the harmony, rather than standing on their own. He was somewhat of a neo-classicist in temperament, striving for a clarity of form, continuity, and craftsmanship. He valued nuance, subtlety, restraint, discretion, naturalness, sincerity, sensibility, an easy sophistication, and elegance. These aesthetic values are reflected in his writing for the voice, rarely going beyond a moderate vocal range. His songs infrequently include extroverted romantic drama. He detested verismo, sentimentality, the superficial, or anything excessive. He worried about repeating himself, but continued to be drawn to the same aesthetic approach throughout his career. It is interesting to note that although Fauré was described as a man with a lively sense of humor by those who knew him, he did not choose to write songs that were overtly witty. Because of various factors, including academic responsibilities, he composed primarily only during summer vacations throughout most of his life.

The songs were performed primarily by the composer's friends and patrons, most often in salons and in performances of the *Societé nationale de musique*. This was a close-knit circle of composers and musicians founded in 1871 by Saint-Saëns, Romain Bussine, Franck, D'Indy, Lalo, Massenet, Bizet, Guiraud, Duparc, and Fauré, with the purpose of furthering the works of the composer-members. Fauré's songs were rarely sung by celebrity singers of the time, especially before 1900. On more than one occasion he cautioned singers not to take his "slow" songs too slowly. Fauré was a good pianist, though not a virtuoso. He was admired as an interpreter of his own work, and loved to accompany his songs throughout his life, even after he was completely deaf. As a pianist, he was described as having powerful hands, a quiet nature at the keyboard, and a clarity of style that was out of fashion with the more dramatic and romantic piano performance style of his time.

Celebrity came late for Fauré. His output, including music in all genres, was known only to a small circle of Parisian society prior to about 1895. At about the age of 50 he began to be recognized more widely in France as a major musical figure. Even at his death he was virtually unknown outside France. His music includes work of consistently high quality for orchestra, for chamber ensembles, and choral works (including the well-known *Requiem*). His opera *Pénélope* is certainly a masterwork, though neglected. Without question is his unqualified place as the quintessential master of French art song. Most would agree that there is no other composer in France's history who more eloquently captured her Gallic voice in song.

Après un rêve

Romain Bussine
(1830-1899)
After an anonymous Tuscan poet

Gabriel Fauré
(1845-1924)

Original key: C minor. Composed 1878? Op. 7, No. 1. The publisher, Hamelle added the opus number, at the request of Fauré, in 1896. Dedicated to Madame Marguerite Baugnies. Published by Choudens, 1878; Hamelle, 1887, first collection, no. 15. First performance, Société nationale de musique, January 11, 1879, Henriette Fuchs, soprano. Romain Bussine, professor of singing at the Paris Conservatoire, adapted the text from an Italian poem titled "Levati sol che la luna é levatai." It is written in an Italianate *bel canto* style, no doubt inspired by Fauré's relationship with the Viardot family. Fauré was engaged to Marianne Viardot, daughter of Pauline Viardot. Marianne terminated the engagement, and Fauré composed this song—the evocation of a lost vision of love—soon after. Fauré's other Italianate settings ("Sérénade toscane," "Barcarolle" and "Chanson du pêcheur") also belong to this period. The popularity of this mélodie has occasioned many instrumental transcriptions.

Après un rêve	After a dream
Dans un sommeil que charmait ton image	In a sleep charmed by your image
Je rêvais le bonheur, ardent mirage;	I dreamed of happiness,
Tes yeux étaient plus doux, ta voix pure et sonore,	Your eyes were soft, your voice pure and rich,
Tu rayonnais comme un ciel éclairé par l'aurore.	You were radiant as a sky lit by the dawn.
Tu m'appelais et je quittais la terre	You called me, and I left the earth
Pour m'enfuir avec toi vers la lumière;	To flee with you towards the light
Les cieux pour nous, entr'ouvraient leurs nues,	The heavens parted their clouds for us
Splendeurs inconnues, lueurs divines entrevues…	Unknown splendors, glimpses of divine light…
Hélas, hélas, triste réveil des songes!	Alas, alas, sad awakening from dreams!
Je t'appelle, ô nuit, rens-moi tes mensonges;	I call to you, o night, give me back your illusions;
Reviens, reviens, radieuse,	Return, return in radiance,
Reviens, ô nuit mystérieuse!	Return, o mysterious night!

Chanson d'amour

Armand Silvestre
(1838-1901)

Gabriel Fauré
(1845-1924)

Original key: F major. Composed 1882. Op. 27, No. 1. Dedicated to Mademoiselle Jane Huré. Published by Hamelle, 1882; second collection, no. 10. First performance: Société nationale de musique, December 9, 1882, Jane Huré, soprano. Armand Silvestre wrote graceful verse often criticized as sentimental and lacking in depth. However, composers such as Fauré and Duparc seemed able to work easily with his poetry. Fauré composed 10 mélodies and a choral work using Silvestre's verses. In this setting, Fauré lengthened the poem by using the first four lines as a refrain.

Chanson d'amour	*Love Song*
J'aime tes yeux, j'aime ton front,	*I love your eyes, I love your forehead,*
O ma rebelle ô ma farouche,	*O my rebel, o my wild one,*
J'aime tes yeux, j'aime ta bouche	*I love your eyes, I love your mouth*
Où mes baisers s'épuiseront.	*Where my kisses will exhaust themselves.*
J'aime ta voix, j'aime l'étrange	*I love your voice, I love the strange*
Grâce de tout ce que tu dis,	*Grace of all you say,*
O ma rebelle, ô mon cher ange,	*O my rebel, o my darling angel*
Mon enfer et mon paradis!	*My hell and my paradise!*
J'aime tout ce qui te fait belle,	*I love everything that makes you beautiful,*
De tes pieds jusqu'à tes cheveux,	*From your feet to your hair,*
O toi vers qui montent mes vœux,	*O you towards whom all my desires fly,*
O ma farouche, ô ma rebelle!	*O my wild one, o my rebel!*

Si mes vers avaient des ailes

Victor Hugo
(1802-1885)

Reynaldo Hahn
(1875-1947)

Composed 1888. No. 2 in the first volume of 20 mélodies (*Premier volume de vingt mélodies*). Published 1895, Heugel. Dedicated to the composer's sister, Maria Hahn. Reynaldo Hahn was Venezuelan by birth, but came to Paris with his family at age four and made a brilliant career in France. He composed this mélodie, perhaps the most familiar of his songs, at age 13. Its fresh charm was clearly influenced by his teacher Jules Massenet. Hahn was a major figure in the cultural life of Paris during the *belle époque*. His mélodies capture the atmosphere of the Parisian salons where Hahn held forth, playing and singing his songs, frequently with a cigarette dangling from his lips. The art of singing was one of his major passions and preoccupations. Recent releases of historic Hahn recordings confirm his voice was small and somewhat bland, but his artistry in shaping musical material is rewarding to hear. He wrote three books on singing (*Du chant, Thèmes variés, L'oreille au guet*), as well as a memoir of Sarah Bernhardt. After 1912, Hahn composed in larger forms: opera, operetta, film music. His operetta *Ciboulette* (1923), perhaps his most famous work, is still performed and recorded.

Si mes vers avaient des ailes	*If my verses had wings*
Mes vers fuiraient, doux et frêles,	*My verses would fly, fragile and gentle,*
Vers votre jardin si beau,	*To your beautiful garden,*
Si mes vers avaient des ailes	*If my verses had wings*
Comme l'oiseau.	*Like a bird!*
Ils voleraient, étincelles,	*They would fly like sparks*
Vers votre foyer qui rit,	*To your cheery hearth,*
Si mes vers avaient des ailes	*If my verses had wings*
Comme l'esprit.	*Like my spirit.*
Près de vous, purs et fidèles,	*Pure and faithful, to your side*
Ils accourraient nuit et jour,	*They would hasten night and day*
Si mes vers avaient des ailes	*If my verses had wings*
Comme l'amour.	*Like love.*

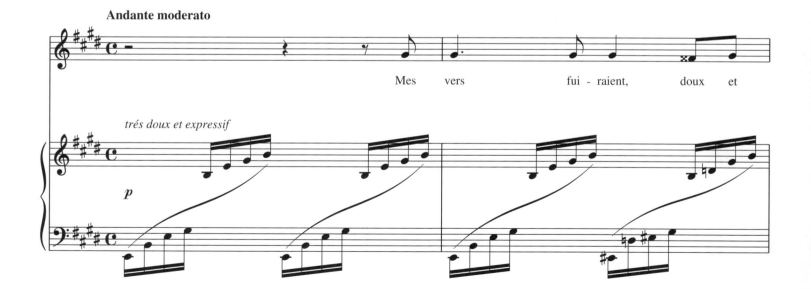

Plaisir d'amour

Jean-Pierre Claris de Florian
(1755-1794)

Johann-Paul Martini
(1741-1816)

This *romance* was composed in 1784 in Nancy, and published the following year as a supplement to the novella *Célestine*. Martini was a German composer who moved to France in 1760 and spent most of his career there. He eventually became well-known for writing opera. He is cited as the first composer in France to compose songs with piano accompaniment rather than continuo. He is most remembered for "Plaisir d'amour," a classic *romance* that remains a famous prototype of the style. The *romance* evolved from earlier French poetic-vocal forms, notably those of the troubadours. The 18th-century *romance* was strophic in form, with simple melodic lines that were sung without affectation. Accompaniments were subordinate to the vocal line and there was little or no musical interaction between voice and piano. "Plaisir d'amour" is notable for its rondo form and more involved accompaniment, which features a prelude, interlude, and postlude.

Plaisir d'amour	The pleasures of love
Plaisir d'amour ne dure qu'un moment,	The pleasures of love last but a moment
Chagrin d'amour dure toute la vie.	The sorrows of love last all life through.
J'ai tout quitté pour l'ingrate Sylvie,	I have given up everything for the ungrateful Sylvia
Elle me quitte et prend un autre amant.	She left me and took another lover.
Plaisir d'amour ne dure qu'un moment,	The pleasures of love last but a moment
Chagrin d'amour dure toute la vie.	The sorrows of love last all life through.
Tant que cette eau coulera doucement	As long as this water runs gently
Vers ce ruisseau qui borde la prairie,	Towards the brook that borders the meadow,
Je t'aimerai, me répétait Sylvie.	I shall love you, Sylvia told me.
L'eau coule encor, elle a changé pourtant.	The stream still flows, but she has changed.
Plaisir d'amour ne dure qu'un moment,	The pleasures of love last but a moment
Chagrin d'amour dure toute la vie.	The sorrows of love last all life through.

Allegretto grazioso

vi - e,

El - le me quitte et prend un autre a -

[rit.]   *p*   [a tempo]

mant.   Plai - sir d'a - mour _____ ne

du - re qu'un mo - ment, _____ Cha - grin d'a -

mour du - re tou - te la vi - - e. _____

Tant que cette eau cou - le -

ra dou - ce - ment Vers

ce ruis - seau qui bor - de la ____ prai - ri - e,

Johannes Brahms

The great German composer Johannes Brahms, master of all genres of concert and recital literature, composed 196 songs for solo voice and piano, with an additional 10 songs adapted for the medium. His lieder span his entire compositional career, from about the age of 18 until his last songs of 1896, though there are years of inactivity. Additionally, Brahms made settings for voice and piano of over 200 German folksongs, most of which were unpublished in his lifetime.

Though Brahms' mentor, Robert Schumann, was himself a master lieder composer, Schubert was Brahms' closest aesthetic predecessor. Both approached composition not as a musico-poetic aesthetic, where poetry is intimately expressed in great detail in music (as was the case with Schumann or Wolf), but more as a compositional reaction to the general emotional mood and content of the poem. Brahms valued music above poetry, and melody over clearly declaimed text. The piano plays an equal but independent role in many of his songs. The musical form of each individual piece had to be perfectly satisfying to him, even if it meant altering the words in some way to suit his design. This way of working made the more dramatic, narrative form of the song cycle (not to mention opera) foreign to his creative temperament.

Brahms' advice to an aspiring song composer was to "make sure that together with your melody you compose a strong, independent bass line." Indeed, an account of Brahms reviewing a young lieder composer's work has him covering all but the vocal line and the bass line with his hands, saying that he could the judge the quality of any song in this manner. Observers noted how prominently Brahms played bass lines of his songs in accompanying singers, reflecting his natural love of counterpoint as a compositional value.

A higher percentage of Brahms' songs were written for a male singer than a female. Brahms went on recital tours as accompanist with his good friend Julius Stockhausen, and wrote many of his greatest songs for this singer. But it is clear that Brahms certainly loved the female voice, since he fell in love with at least four women singers. Many of his songs are on the subject of love. At different times in his life Brahms expressed in his songs the unrequited emotions of his complex relationships with Agathe von Siebold, Elizabeth von Herzogenberg, Rosa Girzick, Hermine Spies, and especially Clara Schumann. On the other hand, most of lyric poetry is about love, so a song composer's work is usually preoccupied with this topic. Nature figures strongly in Brahms' songs. Most characteristic is the nostalgic melancholy and loneliness that seems to permeate so much of his work, especially after his father's death in 1872.

Approximately a quarter of Brahms songs are in simple strophic form. Another quarter are through-composed. Most of the rest are in the form he perfected, something one can term as the varied strophic. Subsequent verses may contain variations in any number of ways to accommodate the subject and character of the progressing poem. "Wie Melodien zieht es mir" and "Vergebliches Ständchen" are examples of varied strophic songs. Sometimes a middle verse will be composed to new music, and the final verse will be a variation on the first, resulting in an ABA form that is still related to the varied strophic, as in the Kugler song "Ständchen."

The compositional dates for Brahms' songs are oftentimes difficult to pin down, for he habitually started something that was not completed in final form for several years. Of song composition he instructed, "Let it rest, let it rest, and keep going back to it until it is completed as a finished work of art, until there is not a note too many or too few, not a bar you can improve on."

Vergebliches Ständchen

Anton Wilhelm Florentin von Zuccalmaglio
(1803-1869)

Johannes Brahms
(1833-1897)

Original key. "For this one song I would sacrifice all the others," wrote Brahms in reply to the praise Eduard Hanslick bestowed upon this work. Brahms was in admittedly high spirits and saw in this exchange between a would-be suitor and haughty maiden many of the traits he admired: a deftly executed folk-like quality, a vibrant melody and active bass line, and not overly subtle humor. Completed in 1882 and published by N. Simrock the same year as Op. 84, No. 4, the poem comes from Zuccalmaglio's 1840 collection *Deutsche Volkslieder*, which contains folk material vastly remodeled by the compiler. Brahms, it appears, believed this was true folk poetry, when in fact, all but a few lines were written by Zuccalmaglio.

Vergebliches Ständchen

(Er)
Guten Abend, mein Schatz,
Guten Abend, mein Kind!
Ich komm aus Lieb zu dir,
Ach, mach mir auf die Tür!

(Sie)
Mein Tür is verschlossen,
Ich laß dich nicht ein;
Mutter, die rät mir klug,
Wärst du herein mit Fug,
Wärs mit mir vorbei!

(Er)
So kalt ist die Nacht,
So eisig der Wind,
Daß mir das Herz erfriert,
Mein Lieb erlöschen wird,
Öffne mir, mein Kind!

(Sie)
Löschet dein Lieb,
Laß sie löschen nur!
Löschet sie immerzu,
Geh heim zu Bett, zur Ruh,
Gute Nacht, mein Knab!

Futile Serenade

(He)
Good evening, my darling,
good evening, my dear!
I'm here out of love for you;
ah, open the door for me!

(She)
My door is locked;
I will not let you in.
Mother counseled me wisely
that if you were permitted to come in
it would be all over for me!

(He)
So cold is the night,
so icy the wind,
that my heart is freezing;
my love will be extinguished.
Open for me, my dear!

(She)
If your love is being extinguished,
just let it go out!
If it keeps going out,
go home to bed, to sleep!
Good night, my lad!

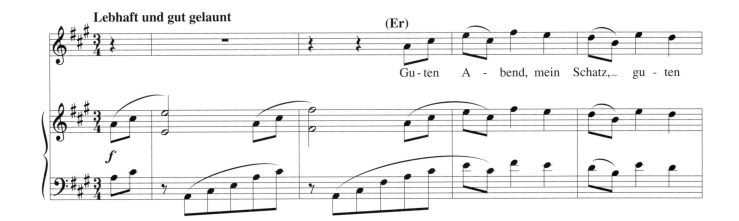

A - bend, mein Kind, gu - ten A - bend, mein Kind!

Ich komm aus Lieb zu— dir, ach, mach mir auf die— Tür, mach mir auf die Tür,

mach mir auf, mach mir auf, mach mir auf— die Tür!

(Sie)

Mein Tür ist ver-schlos-sen, ich laß dich nicht ein,

ich laß dich nicht ein; Mut-ter, die

rät mir klug, wärst du her-ein mit Fug, wärs mit mir vor-bei,

wärs mit mir, wärs mit mir, wärs mit mir vor-bei!

Wie Melodien zieht es mir

Klaus Johann Groth
(1819-1899)

Johannes Brahms
(1833-1897)

Original key: A major. In this poem by Brahms' good friend Groth we find the contemplation of both poetic inspiration and what occurs when that aura of an idea must be solidified in words. The song, Op. 105, No. 1, was composed in August of 1886 while Brahms was vacationing in Switzerland, often in the company of the young contralto, Hermine Spies, who inspired the piece. The opening of the main theme appears also in the first movement of Brahms's Violin Sonata in A major. The song was published by N. Simrock in 1889. Groth's poem is found in his *Hundert Blätter, Paralipomena zum Quickborn* of 1854. It is in standard Hochdeutsche [High German], although Groth's reputation rested largely on his Plattdeutsche [Low German] poetry, the native dialect he and Brahms shared.

Wie Melodien zieht es Mir leise durch den Sinn, Wie Frühlingsblumen blüht es Und schwebt wie Duft dahin.	*Like melodies it pervades my senses softly. Like spring flowers it blooms and drifts along like fragrance.*
Doch kommt das Wort und faßt es Und führt es vor das Aug, Wie Nebelgrau erblaßt es Und schwindet wie ein Hauch.	*But when a word comes and grasps it and brings it before the eye, like gray mist it fades and vanishes like a breath.*
Und dennoch ruht im Reime Verborgen wohl ein Duft, Den mild aus stillem Keime Ein feuchtes Auge ruft.	*And yet there remains in the rhyme a certain hidden fragrance, which gently, from the dormant bud, a tearful eye evokes.*

69

Franz Schubert

The talents of Franz Schubert are well chronicled in any music history source. His nine symphonies, choral pieces, and countless piano and chamber works make him, of course, a major European musical figure, particularly as a transitory talent from the Classical to the Romantic. It is, however, his work as a song composer, producing some 600-plus lieder, which insures him a unique place in history. His song composition began at least as early as age 14 and continued until his death, with some periods of enormous output. In the two-year period of 1815 and 1816 he wrote a remarkable 250 songs.

Schubert reinvented the lied, going much further in the endeavor of setting poetry to music than anyone before him. He created the first substantial body of literature for the vocal recital. His accomplishment, however great, could not have happened without the rise of German lyric poetry by Johann Wolfgang von Goethe, Heinrich Heine, Wilhelm Müller, Ludwig Rellstab, Friedrich Rückert, and Johann Christoph Friedrich von Schiller during the late 18th century and first decades of the 19th century. Schubert also set texts by many minor literary figures, some of which were friends.

Musical success during Schubert's lifetime was measured against Beethoven in the concert hall and Rossini in the opera house. Schubert dreamed of triumph in both places, but never achieved it, almost always failing to find performances of his larger works. As an alternative, the devoted circle of friends around the composer would gather in living rooms and parlors for evenings which came to be called Schubertiads. A majority of the songs were first performed there. These evenings encouraged Schubert in song composition, since there was a ready place, performers and audience for the works. The composer was at the piano regularly in the Schubertiads, accompanying songs and playing piano pieces, but never performed for a wider public. His piano abilities seem to have been adequate but not remarkable. Schubert had many favorite singers, lyric baritone Johann Michael Vogl and soprano Anna Milder Hauptmann among them. On occasion Schubert himself sang a new song for the intimate Schubertiad audience, though he never would have considered himself a singer.

Schubert explored various musical forms in his songs, including strophic, through-composed, freely declamatory, and combined structures. His text setting shines with a balance of sensitivity to words and strong melodic values. The piano accompaniment figures imaginatively reflect the mood and imagery of the texts. Among Schubert's achievements as a song composer is the full flowering of the concept of a narrative song cycle, a group of related poems which tell some kind of story by their progression, shown in the expansive sets *Die Winterreise* and *Die schöne Müllerin*.

Schubert's composition was inspired by many influences. He loved the operas of Gluck, and discovered the baritone Vogl at a performance of *Iphegénie en Tauride*. Schubert also greatly admired Handel, and in his free time played through that composer's operas and oratorios. He thought Mozart's *Don Giovanni* among the very best of all operas, and valued the overture to *Die Zauberflöte* as a masterwork with few peers. As for Beethoven, Schubert held him in high regard. Though they both lived in Vienna, the two never met until 1827, and then briefly, with Beethoven virtually on his deathbed. Five years earlier Schubert dedicated a set of published piano variations to Beethoven and brought a copy to him. The great and famous man was not at home, and humbled by the idea of a return visit, Schubert simply left the new edition. Beethoven apparently approved of the music, and played it nearly every day thereafter with his nephew.

Du bist die Ruh

Friedrich Rückert
(1788-1866)

Franz Schubert
(1797-1828)

Original key. D 776. Rückert, the poet for six of Schubert's songs, was influenced by the Persian poet Hafis (1325-1389) and was a scholar of eastern languages. He taught in both Erlangen and Berlin. When authoring his 1821 collection of poetry titled *Östlichen Rosen* [Eastern Roses] he left the verses untitled, and Schubert therefore gave the name "Du bist die Ruh" to this song. Rückert later gave the poem a title drawn from the third stanza, "Kehr' ein bei mir" [Commune with me]. This song and two others on Rückert texts were published as Op. 59 in September of 1826 by Sauer and Leidesdorf. This text allowed Schubert to group stanzas into a three-part modified strophic form, and the reverent transcendence of the verse finds perfect poise in the music's balance of quietude and intensity.

Du bist die Ruh	You are rest
Du bist die Ruh,	You are rest,
Der Friede mild,	gentle peace;
Die Sehnsucht du,	the longing, you
Und was sie stillt.	and that which satisfies it.
Ich weihe dir	I consecrate to you,
Voll Lust und Schmerz	full of joy and sorrow,
Zur Wohnung hier	as a dwelling place here,
Mein Aug und Herz.	my eyes and heart.
Kehr ein bei mir,	Come commune with me,
Und schließe du	and close
Still hinter dir	quietly behind you
Die Pforten zu.	the gates.
Treib andern Schmerz	Drive other pain
Aus dieser Brust.	from this breast.
Voll sei dies Herz	Full may this heart be
Von deiner Lust.	of your joy.
Dies Augenzelt,	The temple of these eyes
Von deinem Glanz	from your radiance
Allein erhellt,	alone brightens;
O füll es ganz.	oh, fill it completely.

was   sie   stillt.   Ich wei - he dir_____ voll Lust und_ Schmerz

zur Woh - nung hier_____ mein Aug_ und_ Herz,_____ mein Aug und_ Herz._____

Kehr ein bei mir, und schlie - ße du   still hin - ter dir die

o— füll es— ganz,_____ o— füll es— ganz._____

Dies Au - gen - zelt, von dei - nem Glanz al -

lein er - hellt,_____ o— füll es— ganz,_____

o— füll es— ganz._____

Gretchen am Spinnrade

Johann Wolfgang von Goethe
(1749-1832)

Franz Schubert
(1797-1828)

Original key. D 118. Goethe is widely recognized as the greatest figure in German poetry and one of history's towering intellects. His 12,000-line verse drama *Faust*, in which this poem appears as the scene "Gretchens Stube" (Gretchen's Room), was written over a period of some 60 years. Schubert set this text on October 19, 1814, and even as a teenager conjured one of the great miniature masterpieces in all of song literature. This was the first Goethe poem that Schubert set, and was eventually published by Cappi and Diabelli in April of 1821 as Opus 2. In this scene, Gretchen is abandoned by her lover Faust, who has made a pact with the devil, Mephistopheles. The driving spinning wheel motif in the piano and strong harmonic motion contribute to the song's dramatic intensity. Schubert altered the first line of the last verse of the poem on its repeat to "O könnt' ich ihn küssen" (Oh, if I could kiss him). Though Schubert never received the slightest approval or even acknowledgment from Goethe when published songs were sent to him, the composer set 74 of his poems to music.

Gretchen am Spinnrade

Meine Ruh ist hin,
Mein Herz ist schwer,
Ich finde sie nimmer
Und nimmermehr.

Wo ich ihn nicht hab,
Ist mir das Grab,
Die ganze Welt
Ist mir vergällt.

Mein armer Kopf
Ist mir verrückt,
Mein armer Sinn
Ist mir zerstückt.

Nach ihm nur schau ich
Zum Fenster hinaus,
Nach ihm nur geh ich
Aus dem Haus.

Sein hoher Gang,
Sein' edle Gestalt,
Seines Mundes Lächeln,
Seiner Augen Gewalt,

Und seiner Rede
Zauberfluss,
Sein Händedruck,
Und ach, sein Kuss!

Mein Busen drängt
Sich nach ihm hin,
Ach dürft' ich fassen
Und halten ihn,

Und küssen ihn,
So wie ich wollt',
An seinen Küssen
Vergehen sollt'.

Gretchen at the Spinning Wheel

My peace is gone,
my heart is heavy;
I will find it never
and nevermore.

Wherever I do not have him
is for me the grave;
the whole world
is to me loathsome.

My poor head
is deranged;
my poor mind
is shattered.

For him only do I gaze
out from the window;
For him only do I go
out of the house.

His fine gait,
his noble stature,
his mouth's smile,
his eyes' power,

and, of his speech,
magic flow—
his handclasp,
and, ah, his kiss!

My bosom yearns
for him;
ah, could I embrace him
and hold him,

and kiss him
as much as I wish,
in his kisses
I should perish.

Hän - de - druck, und ach, sein Kuss!

Mei - ne Ruh_____ ist hin, mein

Herz_____ ist schwer,_____ ich fin - de, ich

fin - de sie nim - mer und nim - mer -

ihn,_____ so wie_____ ich wollt', an

sei - nen Küs - sen ver - ge - hen

sollt', o könnt'_____ ich ihn küs - sen, so

fz *fz*

wie_____ ich wollt', an sei - nen

fz *fz* *fz*

Richard Strauss

Richard Strauss was a German composer and conductor who made significant contributions to many musical genres, including major compositions for the voice. He was one of the strongest musical influences of the post-Wagner Germany of the late 19th and early 20th centuries. Richard was born on June 11, 1864 in Munich, to a musical family. His father, Franz Strauss, was the principal horn player of the Munich Court Orchestra for nearly 50 years. His mother, Josephine Pschorr, was part of a family of brewers. The Strauss family enjoyed financial independence, and as a result, Richard had a carefree upbringing. He showed musical interest at a very young age. At age four he took piano lessons from August Tombo, and at age eight he took up the violin with Benno Walter, concertmaster of the Munich Court Orchestra. His musical education eventually led him to conducting and composing, assisting the famed Hans von Bülow with his orchestra in Meiningen. Strauss' fame as a composer was assured with the 1889 premiere of his tone poem *Don Juan*, a tremendous success that brought him regard as the most significant and progressive composer since Wagner. Strauss would go on to write many other tone poems including *Don Quixote, Tod und Verklärung, Ein Heldenleben, Also sprach Zarathustra*, and *Til Eulenspiegels lustige Streiche*. His recognition as a world-class conductor during his early career is equally important. Strauss appeared as a guest conductor in Holland, Spain, France, and England in 1897 alone. In 1898 he was appointed chief conductor of the Royal Court Opera in Berlin, where he conducted 71 performances of 25 operas in his first eight-month season. He also conducted Wagner at Bayreuth during his illustrious career. In addition to his work as a composer and conductor, Strauss was a tireless champion of composer's rights and he campaigned for seven years to revise German copyright law to pay royalties to composers for performance and publication of their works.

While Strauss' symphonic masterpieces brought him great recognition, it was to opera that he would primarily turn after 1898. His first opera, *Guntram*, was a failure, but Strauss followed that up with the successful *Feuersnot*. Nothing could prepare theatregoers, however, for Strauss' next project. *Salome*, with its overt sexuality and gruesome content, caused an immediate scandal at its 1905 premiere in Dresden. With the controversy came free publicity, and *Salome* was produced in 50 opera houses in the two years following its premiere. Strauss would write operas for most of the rest of his life, including *Elektra, Der Rosenkavalier, Ariadne auf Naxos, Die Frau ohne Schatten, Intermezzo, Die ägyptische Helena, Arabella, Die schweigsame Frau, Friedenstag, Daphne, Die Liebe der Danae*, and *Capriccio*. After *Elektra*, his aesthetic style retreated to a more conservative approach, where he remained the rest of his career.

Amid the large works, Strauss was also an active lieder composer for most of his career. Strauss' ability to write for the voice, strikingly apparent in his operas, is evident in his many songs. Strauss composed over 200 songs during his lifetime, the majority of which he wrote between 1885 and 1906. It is apparent that Strauss the song composer paved the way for Strauss the opera composer. A 12-year hiatus in song composition ended in 1918, and Strauss composed songs until his final work in the 1940s, though he never achieved the pace of song output as the period before 1900. In his early lieder he was undoubtedly inspired to write for the voice after meeting and eventually marrying Pauline de Ahna, a renowned German soprano. They met in 1894 when Pauline sang Elisabeth in Wagner's *Tannhäuser* with Strauss conducting at Bayreuth. Many of Strauss' songs were written with her voice in mind; Strauss gave the songs of Op. 27 to Pauline as a wedding gift. He wrote 31 songs in six collections during 1899-1901 alone.

Though Strauss was himself a competent pianist, he wrote very little literature for the instrument. The song accompaniments are our best understanding of Strauss as a composer for piano. His piano accompaniments partner equally with the voice and characterize the general mood of the text being sung. The piano accompaniments also tend to be orchestral in nature, with broad, sweeping gestures or exquisitely delicate colors. It was a logical progression then that Strauss developed the lied with orchestra further than any composer before him. He orchestrated 27 of his songs originally written for voice and piano, and composed 15 songs directly for voice and orchestra. While Strauss, a brilliant orchestrator, was naturally drawn to the orchestral lied as a genre, there was a practical reason as well. He orchestrated many of his songs specifically for concerts which he conducted with his wife Pauline as soloist during the 1890s.

Influences range from Mozart to Wagner in a style that is unmistakably Straussian. As with his operas, Strauss is able to lucidly depict characters through his songs, utilizing effective text setting and richly descriptive piano accompaniments. Strauss grew up in a musical culture heavily influenced by Wagner. Both composers shared a strong sense of harmonic tension and resolution sustained over long phrases. Strauss' lieder are more compact than the larger works, and hence less spacious in harmony and form, but they still contain the characteristic sureness of harmonic direction and arching phrases. Strauss nearly always wrote vocal music, including opera, with the lyric voice as his inspiration, as Mozart did. This contrasts with Wagner, who most often composed with larger, more dramatic voices in mind. As most of Strauss' songs were originally performed in the concert hall, they have a distinct style that differs clearly from lieder composed for the salon or other intimate venues. In general, the songs are musically conservative, rarely moving to the modern "decadence" of *Salome* and *Elektra*.

Breit' über mein Haupt

Adolph Friedrich von Schack
(1815-1894)

Richard Strauss
(1864-1949)

Original key. Completed in 1888, this song was published the same year. Unusually diatonic for Strauss, the piece retains a serene and radiant mood throughout. The poet Schack was a wealthy aristocrat who was an active art critic and patron as well as a translator of Persian literature. His poetry was appreciated by the Naturalists, which is easy to understand when one notes the realistic, sensual details of this verse.

Breit' über mein Haupt	*Spread out over my head*
Breit' über mein Haupt dein schwarzes Haar,	*Spread over my head your black hair,*
Neig' zu mir dien Angesicht,	*draw your face closer to me,*
Da strömt in die Seele so hell und klar	*there flows into my soul so bright and clear*
Mir deiner Augen Licht.	*your eyes' light.*
Ich will nicht droben der Sonne Pracht,	*I do not wish for the sun's magnificence above,*
Noch der Sterne leuchtenden Kranz,	*nor even the stars shining garland,*
Ich will nur deiner Locken Nacht,	*I wish only for the night of your locks,*
Und deiner Blicke Glanz.	*and the light of your eyes.*

Wolfgang Amadeus Mozart

The great Wolfgang Amadeus Mozart was a master of any form he chose, including the occasional solo song. The art song was not a developed genre during his lifetime. Mozart's songs number only about 30 among an enormous output of opera, symphonies, choral works and chamber music. The lieder movement of 19th-century Germany and Austria, which championed romantic ideals in its personal poetry by masters such as Goethe, Rückert, and Heine, had not taken hold yet during Mozart's lifetime. By the mid-18th century, vocal music accompaniments had evolved from being realized at sight from figured bass by a performer to being fully written out by a composer. Later in that century, songs were usually written by minor composers, and were almost always strophic in form, with the voice line often in an uninspired, serviceable melody, closely mirrored in the piano accompaniment. Prior to Mozart's work, few songs treated the voice and piano independently and equally.

The pianoforte of Mozart's day was a new instrument, just beginning to provide the dynamic and emotional range necessary to play a concerto with orchestra, or to adequately accompany an expressive vocal or chamber performance. The rise in popularity of the piano in the decades after Mozart's death contributed to a culture ready for salon concerts perfect for lieder.

Mozart's songs were generally intended for home entertainment. They were not commissioned, but composed as gifts for hosts, friends or colleagues, or as romantic gestures. There were many singers in Mozart's circle of friends and family, including his wife and sister-in-law. His understanding of the voice as an instrument comes through in music written for those voices he knew best. Though there was little, if any, money to be made from songs in his time, Mozart still continued planning such compositions at various times throughout his life, though he viewed them as incidental pieces. Even the very existence of Mozart's songs reveals his love for the voice and piano.

The texts Mozart used for his songs were often casually chosen, written by friends or lesser-known poets. Mozart composed songs primarily to German words, with an occasional Italian or French text. Except for one setting of Goethe ("Das Veilchen"), he did not seek out high literature to set to music. Mozart's compositional style, with a strong sense of musical form, instead gravitated to simpler texts that could be molded to his musical design. The composer's often quoted philosophy about word-setting was stated in a letter to his father about the libretto for *Die Entführung aus dem Serail*: "…the poetry must be altogether the obedient daughter of the music…when music reigns supreme and one listens to it, all else is forgotten."

Most of Mozart's earliest songs were simple strophic works in the tradition of folksongs. Occasionally a simple arietta reminiscent of an opera aria was composed, such as "Ridente la calma," Mozart's only *da capo* song in Italian. Mozart's later songs were written around the same time as the Lorenzo Da Ponte operas, *Le Nozze di Figaro*, *Don Giovanni*, and *Così fan tutte*. These songs are through-composed and sometimes have the same kind of accompanied recitative style that is commonly heard in these Mozart operas. Some of his works hint toward mature lieder, with an intimate union of poetry and music, such as "Abendempfindung."

Despite the minor place song plays in Mozart's work, every piece he created bears the exquisite taste, natural craft and elegance of a master composer. The songs are also fascinating as a distilled concept of vocal melody by one of the greatest of melodists.

Das Veilchen

Johann Wolfgang von Goethe
(1749-1832)

Wolfgang Amadeus Mozart
(1756-1791)

Original key. K. 476. With this text, Mozart linked his name for the only time with that of the great German poet and author Goethe. Goethe's enormous output is testament to his artistry and intellect. The Weimar Edition of his works runs to 133 volumes of plays, poetry, novels, scientific treatises, a correspondence with the poet Schiller, and the great drama *Faust*, written over a period of some 60 years. Mozart completed this song on June 8, 1785, and it was published in Vienna in 1789. He departs from the strictly strophic design favored in his time to create a flexible setting for each verse, and the sculpted vocal lines along with the sensitivity and interest in the piano accompaniment point to developments that would be solidified in art song of the early 19th century.

Das Veilchen	The Violet
Ein Veilchen auf der Wiese stand,	A violet stood in the meadow,
Gebückt in sich und unbekannt;	cowering and unseen;
Es war ein herzigs Veilchen.	it was a charming violet.
Da kam ein' junge Schäferin	There came a young shepherdess,
Mit leichtem Schritt und munterm Sinn	with a light step and a cheerful heart
Daher, daher,	that way, that way,
Die Wiese her und sang.	along the meadow and sang.
»Ach,« denkt das Veilchen, »wär' ich nur	"Ah," thinks the violet, "were I only
Die schönste Blume der Natur,	the most beautiful flower in nature,
Ach, nur ein kleines Weilchen,	ah, only for a little while,
Bis mich das Liebchen abgepflückt	until the sweetheart plucked me
Und an dem Busen matt gedrückt,	and on her bosom pressed me flat,
Ach nur, ach nur	ah only, ah only
Ein Viertelstündchen lang!«	for a quarter-hour!"
Ach! Aber ach! das Mädchen kam	Ah! but alas! the girl came
Und nicht in acht das Veilchen nahm,	and did not take notice of the violet,
Ertrat das arme Veilchen.	trampled on the poor violet.
Es sank und starb und freut' sich noch:	It sank and died, yet rejoiced for itself:
»Und sterb' ich denn, so sterb' ich doch	"And if I die, at least I die,
Durch sie, durch sie,	because of her, because of her,
Zu ihren Füßen doch.«	right at her feet."
Das arme Veilchen!	The poor violet!
Es war ein herzigs Veilchen.	It was a charming violet.

her, die Wie - se her und sang.

»Ach,« denkt das Veil - chen, »wär' ich nur die schön - ste Blu - me der Na - tur, ach, nur ein klei - nes Weil - chen, bis mich das Lieb - chen

Ridente la calma

Anonymous

Wolfgang Amadeus Mozart
(1756-1791)

Original key. K. 210a. Mozart's only song in this style. The chronology of the composition of "Ridente la calma" is unclear. Wolfgang embarked on a trip to Italy with his father in 1770, one of the many musical tours that he and his family would take during his childhood. While traveling, Wolfgang encountered many significant musicians, including Sammartini. He also made the acquaintance of Josef Mysliveček, a Czech composer known at the time for his operas. The first section of "Ridente la calma" appears in an aria by Mysliveček entitled "Il mio caro bene, attendo, sospiro." It is generally accepted that Mozart adapted this piece into "Ridente la calma," utilizing a different text, and altering the middle section and the ending. It was originally catalogued as K. 152, and later renumbered as K. 210a. The song is in an Italianate *da capo* aria style. Mysliveček's aria dates from 1773 or 1774, with Mozart's version possibly appearing around 1775, though this cannot be confirmed. This is a jewel-like arietta, a song in the style of a simple operatic aria of the period. Mozart may have written the arietta for voice and orchestra, and subsequently created a piano reduction.

Ridente la calma	*Pleasant is the calm*
Ridente la calma nell'alma si desti;	*Pleasant is the calm in my being;*
Né resti più segno di sdegno e timor.	*No trace of disdain and fear remain.*
Tu vieni, frattanto, a stringer mio bene,	*You come meanwhile to grasp, my love,*
Le dolce catene sí grate al mio cor.	*the sweet chains that make grateful my heart.*

*appoggiatura possible

Né re-sti un se-gno di sde-gno e ti-

mor. Ri-den-te la cal-ma nell' al-ma si

de-sti; Né re-sti più se-gno di sde-gno e ti-

mor, Né re-sti più se-gno di sde-gno e ti-

gra - te al mio cor. Ri - den - te la cal - ma nell'_____

al - ma _____ si _____ de - sti, nell' _____ al - ma si _____

de - sti; Né re - sti un

se - gno di sde - gno e ti - mor. Ri - den - te la

L'abbandono
(Romanza)

Anonymous

Vincenzo Bellini
(1801-1835)

Original key. Vincenzo Bellini was born on November 3, 1801 in Catania, Sicily. His musical family recognized and encouraged his talents, with the young Vincenzo composing his first complete piece at the tender age of six. Vincenzo's musical education was the responsibility of his father and grandfather. In 1819 his family sent him to the Real Collegio di Musica in Naples to complete his formal music education. It was there that Bellini's career as an opera composer was born. His opera *Adelson e Salvini* was premiered at the school in 1825, and its success led to a commission for his next opera, *Bianca e Fernando* (later renamed *Bianca e Gernando*). His collaboration with librettist Felice Romani began with the premiere of *Il pirata* at La Scala in 1827. The Bellini/Romani partnership produced six more operas, including *I Capuleti e i Montecchi*, *Norma*, and *La sonnambula*, three of Bellini's best-known works. Bellini's final opera, *I puritani*, premiered in Paris on January 24, 1835. Bellini lived in Paris for the remainder of his short life, dying of an intestinal ailment on September 23, 1835.

Bellini is most known for his 10 operas, though his output as a composer includes pieces for voice and piano. Most of his instrumental and sacred works were written prior to the premiere of his first opera in 1825, with the majority of his songs being written after 1825. "L'abbandono" was originally published for mezzo-soprano and piano. It was also included in Bellini's unfinished opera *Ernani* as a duet between Elvira and Don Carlo. Bellini's compositional style is the epitome of pure, romantic Italian vocal melody, known as *bel canto* (beautiful singing).

L'abbandono

The abandonment

Solitario zeffiretto,
A che movi i tuoi sospiri?

Solitary little wind,
to whom are you sending your sighs?

Il sospiro a me sol lice,
Chè, dolente ed infelice,
Chiamo Dafne che non ode
L'insoffribil mio martir.

The sighing is left to me alone
because, grieving and miserable,
I cry out to Dafne, who does not hearken to
my insufferable torment.

Langue invan la mammolette
E la rosa e il gelsommino;
Lunge son da lui che adoro,
Non conosco alcun ristoro
Se non viene a consolarmi
Col bel guardo cilestrino.

Vainly languish the tiny violet
and the rose and the jasmine;
far am I from him whom I adore.
I feel no contentment
if he does not come to relieve me
with his radiant sky blue eyes.

Ape industre, che vagando
Sempre vai di fior in fiore,
Ascolta.

Industrious bee, who is voyaging
always from flower to flower,
listen:

Se lo scorgi ov'ei dimora,
Di' che rieda a chi l'adora,
Come riedi tu nel seno
Delle rose al primo albor.

If you see him wherever he is living
tell him that he may come back to the one who adores him,
like you return to the breast
of the rose at the break of dawn.

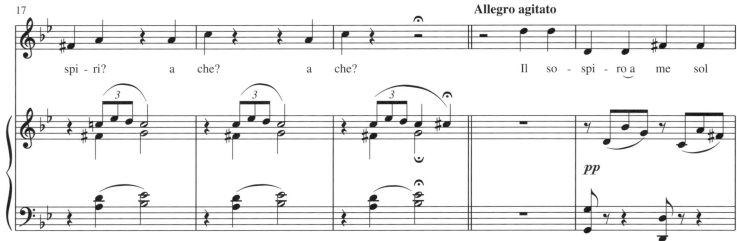

Intorno all'idol mio
from
ORONTEA

Anonymous

Antonio (Pietro) Cesti
(1623-1669)

Antonio Cesti was one of the most celebrated Italian opera composers of his time. Though he did not spend a lot of time in Venice, his style is typically Venetian, in the operatic style of Cavalli. Pietro served as a choirboy in Arezzo. He took on the name Antonio upon joining the Franciscan order in 1637. His life as a priest often came in conflict with his life as a composer; he was rebuked on numerous occasions by his order in Arezzo for his "dishonorable and irregular life." Cesti is said to have written over 100 operas, but only 15 have survived. The most prominent are *Orontea* (1649), *La Dori* (1661), and *Il pomo d'oro* (1667). Unlike the adventuresome chromaticism of Monteverdi or Cavalli, Cesti's music rarely strays from simple harmonic progressions. It instead relies on smoother contours and regular, often sequential patterns, rather than stressing rhythmic play. This realization/arrangement by Alessandro Parisotti, originally published by Ricordi in the 1880s, introduced this song into the modern repertoire. Though Parisotti's editions do not conform to current early music scholarship, they are lyrical, compelling, and historical in their own right.

Intorno all'idol mio	*Around my idol*
Intorno all'idol mio	*Around my idol*
spirate pur, spirate,	*blow, only blow,*
aure soavi e grate;	*breezes mild and pleasant;*
e nelle guancie elette	*and on the blessed cheeks*
baciatelo per me,	*kiss him for me,*
cortesi aurette!	*kind winds!*
Al mio ben, che riposa	*To my love, who slumbers*
su l'ali della quiete,	*on the wings of quiet,*
grati sogni assistete.	*grant gracious dreams.*
E il mio racchiuso ardore	*And my cloaked ardor*
svelate gli per me,	*unveil to him for me,*
o larve d'amore!	*o angels of love!*

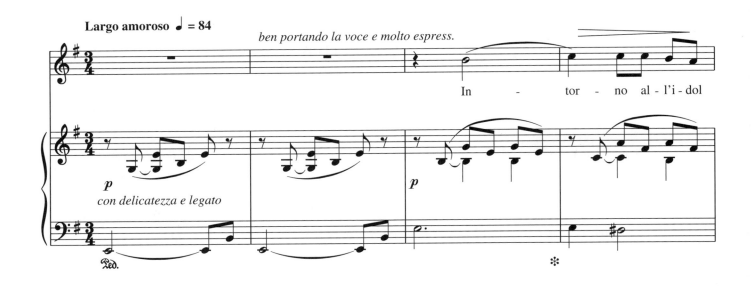

Realization/arrangement by Allessandro Parisotti

Al mio ben, __ che ri - po - sa su

l'a - li __ del - la qui - e - te, gra - ti,

gra - ti __ so - gni as - si - ste - te __ E il

mio rac - chiu - so ar - do - re sve - la - te - gli per me, __ o __

Come l'allodoletta

Alberto Donaudy
(1880-1941)

Stefano Donaudy
(1879-1925)

Original key. Italian composer Stefano Donaudy was born in Palermo, on the island of Sicily, on February 21, 1879, and died in Naples on the mainland on May 30, 1925. Donaudy is remembered for his charming Italian songs. Stefano's talent surfaced early. His first opera, *Folchetto*, premiered in Palermo in 1892, when Donaudy was only 13 years old. Donaudy's other operas include *Scampagnata* (1898), *Theodor Körner* (1902), *Sperduti nel buio* (1907), *Ramuntcho* (1921), and *La Fiamminga* (1922). Donaudy's younger brother Alberto (1880-1941) collaborated with him on many projects, co-writing the libretto with Roberto Bracco for *Sperduti nel buio* and writing the libretto for *Theodor Körner*. This opera was based on the life of Körner, a German poet and revolutionary in the time of Napoleon. The Donaudy brothers followed numerous composers, most notably Franz Schubert, in their treatment of Körner's poems and life in music. Donaudy also composed a symphonic poem titled *Le Rêve*.

Most of Donaudy's output has been forgotten today, but his songs are still popular. First published by Ricordi in two volumes in 1918 and 1922 under the name *Arie di stille antico* (Arias in Antique Style), these 36 songs have texts written by Donaudy's brother Alberto. The term "antico" (antique) refers not to the period in which they were written, but rather to Donaudy's use of older song forms, like the arie, arietta, ballatella, canzone, canzonetta, frottola, madrigal, maggiolata, and villanella. These lushly romantic songs have been recorded by singers from Enrico Caruso to Andrea Bocelli.

Come l'allodoletta

Come l'allodoletta per li prati,
così fugge la pace e l'allegranza
da un cor gentile in cui sol regna amore!

Passa ogni gioia, passa ogni dolzore
da un cor gentile in cui sol regna amore;
e l'alma che ne sente la gravanza,
sen' muore di gelo come un fior!

As the little lark

As the little lark over the fields,
so flees rest and bliss
from a kind heart in which only love reigns!

Every joy, every happiness passes
from a kind heart in which only love reigns!
and the soul which endures the weight of it
dies of frost, like a flower!

Andantino un poco lento

sentito
p

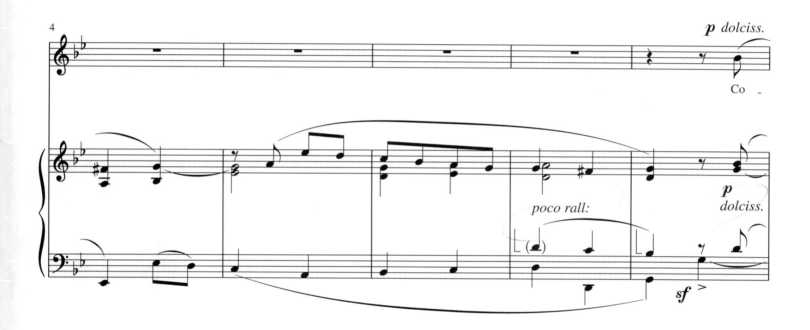

p dolciss.

Co -

poco rall:

p
dolciss.

sf

me l'al - lo - do - let - ta per li pra - ti, co -

El majo discreto

from *Colección de tonadillas*

Fernando Periquet
(1873-1940)

Enrique Granados
(1867-1916)

Enrique Granados was Catalan by birth. His family moved to Barcelona, where he began his musical studies. A scholarship allowed Granados to spend two years as an "auditeur" at the Paris Conservertoire. His first success as a composer came in Madrid with the premiere of his first opera, *María del Carmen*, in 1898. In 1909 Granados began work on the piano suite *Goyescas*, with which he achieved international recognition in 1914 after its Paris premiere. This piece was expanded into an opera, which was premiered at the Metropolitan Opera in New York in 1916. Its success resulted in an invitation for Granados to perform for President Wilson in Washington, D.C. On his trip back to Europe, the ship on which he returned was torpedoed in the English Channel. Granados was rescued but then drowned in a desperate and futile attempt to save his wife. Granados' music is rooted in a blend of Spanish nationalism, Spanish historical musical characteristics and European compositional tradition. His major contributions to vocal literature are the 12 *Tonadillas* of 1910-1911, inspired both by the theme of romantic love and etchings of Francisco Goya, though it is not a cycle in the true sense of the word.

El majo discreto	The discreet majo
Dicen que mi majo es feo.	They say my man is ugly.
Es posible que sí que lo sea,	It is possible that if he is,
Que amor es deseo que ciega y marea.	that love is desire that blinds and upsets.
Ha tiempo que sé que quien ama no ve.	For awhile I've known a lover doesn't see.
Mas si no es mi majo un hombre	But if my lover is not aman
que por lindo descuelle y asombre,	that for his beauty stands out and amazes,
en cambio es discreto y guarda un secreto	but is discreet and keeps a secret
que yo posé en él sabiendo que es fiel.	that I rest in him knowing that he is loyal.
¿Cuál es el secreto que el majo guardó?	What is the secret that he kept?
Sería indiscreto contarlo yo.	It would be indiscreet to tell.
No poco trabajo costara saber	Not a little work would it take to know
secretos de un majo con una mujer.	secrets of a man with a woman.
Nació en Lavapies.	He was born in Lavapies.
¡Eh! ¡Eh! ¡Es un majo, un majo es!	Eh! Eh! He is a majo, a majo is he.

mi ___ ma - jo un hom - bre que por lin - do ___ des - cue - lle ___ y a -

som - bre, en cam - bio es dis - cre - to ___ y guar - da un se - cre - to que

yo po - sé en él ___ sa - bien ___ do ___ que es fiel.

¿Cuál

Del cabello más sutil

from *Canciones clásicas españolas*

Anonymous

Fernando Obradors
(1897-1945)

Spanish composer Fernando Obradors often looked to the past for inspiration. His success was due to an ability to capitalize on the popular concepts of what constitutes a "Spanish song," setting many classic folksongs for voice and piano. He was born in Barcelona and was self-taught in harmony, counterpoint and composition and studied piano with his mother. He was the conductor of the Liceo and Radio Barcelona Orchestras and the Philharmonic Orchestra of Gran Canaria. While Obradors wrote *zarzuela* (an extremely popular form of Spanish musical theater) and symphonic works, his best-known music is the *Canciones clásicas españolas* (Classic Spanish Songs).

Del cabello más sutil	*Of the hair most delicate*
Del cabello más sutil	*Of the hair most delicate*
Que tienes en tu trenzado	*that you have in your braids,*
He de hacer una cadena	*I have to make a chain*
Para traerte a mi lado.	*to bring you to my side.*
Una alcarraza en tu casa,	*A jug in your house,*
Chiquilla, quisiera ser,	*darling, I would like to be*
Para besarte en la boca,	*to kiss you on the mouth*
Cuando fueras a beber.	*when you went to drink.*
¡Ah!